My Little Golden Book About

KAMALA HARRIS

By Rajani LaRocca

Illustrated by Ashley Evans

A GOLDEN BOOK • NEW YORK

 Published in the United States by Golden Books,
an imprint of Random House Children's Books, a division of Penguin Random House LLC,
1745 Broadway, New York, NY 10019. Golden Books, A Golden Book, A Little Golden Book,
the G colophon, and the distinctive gold spine are registered trademarks of
Penguin Random House LLC.
rhcbooks.com
Educators and librarians, for a variety of teaching tools, visit us at RHTeachersLibrarians.com
Library of Congress Control Number: 2021930923
ISBN 978-0-593-43022-4 (trade) — ISBN 978-0-593-43023-1 (ebook)
Printed in the United States of America
10 9 8 7 6 5 4 3 2 1

KAMALA DEVI HARRIS IS THE FIRST BLACK PERSON, FIRST SOUTH ASIAN AMERICAN, AND FIRST WOMAN VICE PRESIDENT OF THE UNITED STATES.

Kamala was born in Oakland, California, on October 20, 1964. Her parents were immigrants. Kamala's mother was a scientist from India, and her father was an economist from Jamaica.

Kamala's parents separated when she was young, and Kamala and her sister, Maya, were raised mostly by their mother, who taught them to be "conscious and compassionate about the struggles of all people."

While growing up, Kamala attended both a Black Baptist church and a Hindu temple.

In kindergarten, Kamala was one of many Black students who were bused from their poorer neighborhood to a school in a wealthier part of town. When Kamala and Maya went to visit their father on weekends, there were kids in that neighborhood who were not allowed to play with them because they were Black.

Kamala's mom got a job in Canada, so the family moved there when Kamala was twelve. It was hard to leave sunny California to go to a place where the winters were cold and snowy.

Her family lived in an apartment complex that didn't allow kids to play on the lawn. Kamala and Maya held a protest, and the rule was changed.

Kamala made close friends at school in Canada, and even formed a dance group. But she missed her home—the United States.

Let us Play!
The lawn is for everyone!

Kamala returned to the United States for college. She went to Howard University, a historically Black university in Washington, DC. She joined the debate team and the Alpha Kappa Alpha sorority, where she organized service projects.

She continued to participate in protests against injustice.

After graduating from Howard, Kamala went to law school.

For her first job out of law school, Kamala became a prosecutor, representing the people of California in court against those who broke the law. She focused on helping women and children who were victims of crime.

In 2003, Kamala became the district attorney, or top prosecutor, of San Francisco. She was the first Black woman and first South Asian woman in California to be elected to this position.

Eight years later, Kamala was elected attorney general of California—the highest law office in the state.

During her time in that role, Kamala worked to protect California's homeowners, the environment, women's rights, and LGBTQ+ rights. She also helped make the police more accountable for their actions.

WOMEN'S
MARCH

In 2014, Kamala married lawyer Doug Emhoff and became stepmom to his two children, Cole and Ella, who lovingly call her "Momala."

Kamala loves to cook for her family and friends. She grew up eating dal, yogurt, and spiced vegetables that her mom prepared, and she started cooking as a kid, making scrambled eggs topped with cheese in the shape of a smiley face. Now her favorite foods include tuna melts, different kinds of beans, and roast chicken with lemon and herbs.

Kamala exercises every day, and has a collection of her favorite sneakers, Converse Chuck Taylors, in many colors.

In 2016, Kamala was elected United States senator for California, becoming the second Black woman (the first from California) and the first South Asian American to be elected to the U.S. Senate.

During her Senate career, Kamala defended the rights of immigrants and questioned witnesses. She also spoke on the floor of the Senate about the fact that no one is above the law, including the president, during the first impeachment trial of President Donald Trump.

KAMAL
F
PRES

In January 2019, Kamala announced that she was running for president of the United States. She talked about issues that were important to her, including civil rights, anti-racism, women's rights, and getting health care for everyone in the United States. Lots of people supported Kamala for president, but over time it became clear that she would not win the nomination. She ended her campaign and encouraged people to vote for fellow Democrat Joe Biden.

Soon after, Kamala accepted Joe Biden's offer to be his vice presidential candidate. Once again, Kamala was the first: the first African-American and first South Asian American to be named the vice presidential candidate for one of the two major political parties. She was also the third woman.

Kamala said she believes strongly in the values her mother taught her, a "vision of our nation as a beloved community—where all are welcome, no matter what we look like, no matter where we come from or who we love."

That November, Joe Biden and Kamala Harris were declared the winners of the election. She wore white the night of the announcement in honor of those who had fought to get women the right to vote—something that had happened only a hundred years earlier.

During her victory speech, Kamala talked about her mother and "the generations of women—Black women, Asian, white, Latina, Native American women who throughout our nation's history have paved the way for this moment tonight. Women who fought and sacrificed so much for equality, liberty and justice for all."

On January 20, 2021, a historic day, Kamala took the oath of office as vice president of the United States. She continues to fight for the rights of all Americans. And she said, "While I may be the first woman in this office, I won't be the last!"